T0349796

F**K FLYING

F**K FLYING

101
eco-friendly ways
to travel

First published in Great Britain in 2020 by Trapeze
An imprint of Orion Publishing Group Ltd
Carmelite House, 50 Victoria Embankment, London, EC4Y 0DZ

An Hachette UK Company

1 3 5 7 9 10 8 6 4 2

Text © The Orion Publishing Group Ltd 2020
Illustrations by Emanuel Santos

The right of The Orion Publishing Group Ltd to be identified
as the author of this work has been asserted in accordance
with the Copyright, Designs and Patents Act 1988.

All rights reserved. No part of this publication may be
reproduced, stored in a retrieval system, or transmitted in any
form or by any means, electronic, mechanical, photocopying,
recording or otherwise, without the prior permission of both
the copyright owner and the above publisher.

A CIP catalogue record for this book is available from the British Library.

Hardback ISBN: 978 1 4091 9966 3
eBook ISBN: 978 1 4091 9967 0

Printed and bound in Great Britain by Clays Ltd, Elcograf S.p.A.

Every effort has been made to fulfil requirements with regard to
reproducing copyright material. The author and publisher will be
glad to rectify any omissions at the earliest opportunity.

www.orionbooks.co.uk

CONTENTS

Introduction   1

The 101 ways:
Everyday Travelling   7
Planning   33
Packing   59
To Fly or Not to Fly?   75
When You Get There   97

References   121

INTRODUCTION

Where to begin?

Every day we're travelling. Whether it's popping to the shops, commuting to work or setting off on holiday, we're on the move all the time. So, it makes sense that one of the most powerful and impactful changes we can make to help save the planet is rethinking how we get from A to B.

Globally, around 74 million cars are sold each year and it has been estimated that by 2035 there will 2 billion cars on our roads.[1] That's a *lot* of cars. Similarly, we take approximately 40.3 million flights a year worldwide – and the world has become a more connected place and travelling has never been easier.[2]

However, moving around more has come with a cost. Every time we use a vehicle with a motor (cars, motorbikes, buses, coaches, boats and planes), greenhouse gases are produced. Mostly this is carbon dioxide and these emissions contribute to global warming.

Typically, the way we travel has involved one of these

motorised forms of transport and this is especially evident in the tourist industry. Studies have estimated that this sector contributes between 5 and 6% of global emissions, of which three quarters (4% in total) comes from transport, including 40% (2.5% of the total) from aviation, 23% (1.5% total) from cars and 21% (1% total) from accommodation.[3] Of course, this is a huge carbon footprint; however, it's also a huge opportunity for change.

The debate on flying

It's estimated that 8.2 billion of us will take a flight in 2037.[4] Blimey. Not only does this mean there will be a lot of postcards getting lost in the international post, but it also poses a big threat to our environment. To put it into some context, the carbon footprint of a return trip from London to Rome (on average two and a half hours direct) creates more carbon emissions (234kg per passenger) than the average emissions produced by citizens of seventeen countries annually.[5] That's staggering and cause for a pause in how we think and behave.

Of course, the simplest 'solution' in the face of these statistics is to simply say 'no!' to flying and many people are doing just this. Online and in the media, more and more people are harnessing the power of the Swedish term *flygsham* ('flight shame') to embrace a no-flying lifestyle.

The Swedish 'No-Fly' campaign is set to have over 100,000 pledges by the end of 2020 and across the world people are taking on the #flyfree challenge.

But what do you do if you have to fly? Maybe you've got a business meeting you need to attend? Or you have family who live abroad? Perhaps you've always dreamed of visiting a distant country – is that no longer a possibility?

Does offsetting work?

A widely used term you'll hear when you get stuck into the sustainable travel debates, is 'carbon offsetting'. So, what does it mean?

The theory behind carbon offsetting is that for the emissions you produce by travelling from one place to another, you counter by contributing to a project that is designed to reduce the carbon dioxide in our atmosphere by the same amount. A common example is reforestation. It's a snazzy idea and it's frequently being offered to airline passengers as a way of offsetting the environmental costs of their flight.

But it's not a completely flawless system. Unfortunately, offsetting doesn't reduce carbon emissions and so isn't going to solve the problem of our carbon footprint long-term. Furthermore, some argue that by embracing offsetting, we're reducing the incentive on companies to innovate. By shifting the responsibility onto the consumer from the manufacturer, we're slowing the drive to create greener travel options.

It's also worth considering that while reforestation is also a positive step, planting new trees doesn't replace the habitats and biodiversity that the previous forests supplied. Alarmingly, deforestation and forest degradation are the second biggest causes of global warning (15%) and are the largest causes in some countries, such as Brazil and Indonesia.[6]

Ultimately, it's a complex issue and the best thing you can do is to read more on the subject and figure out what works best for you. Taking action in some way is better than taking no action at all.

What can we do?

Across the world there are brilliant initiatives being put in place to raise awareness and act against unsustainable travel. Undoubtedly, Greta Thunberg, the teenage Swedish activist, did much to bring the topic to global attention when she sailed to the UN climate conference in New York in a zero-emissions yacht instead of flying.

But there are more changes being made all over the world:

- ⊕ Prince Harry has launched Travalsyt, a sustainable travel and tourism initiative.

- ⊕ In the UK, the selling of petrol, diesel and hybrid cars will be made illegal from 2035.

- ⊕ Germany runs a National Competition for Sustainable Tourism Destination.

- ⊕ In Paris, the introduction of compulsory anti-pollution stickers and a ban on these vehicles from 8am to 8pm Monday to Friday, has led to a 6.05% drop in cars during its first six months.

There's so much more going on and change starts here, with you. Together, we can make a difference. Whether it's a big change, like having a fly-free year, or a smaller change, like walking or cycling to the shops instead of driving, *everyone* can do something.

So, let's get cracking, shall we?

EVERYDAY

TRAVELLING

#1 Be there in 30

If you're going to take away one tip from this little book, make sure it's this one: before you go anywhere, think 30! Will it take you 30 minutes to walk (or cycle, if you're comfortable on a bike) there? Yes? Well, it's time to plug in to your favourite podcast or album and get moving.

#2 The Bus is Boss

Pollution from transport makes up around 25 per cent of the UK's total greenhouse gas emissions,[7] so it goes without saying that taking the bus instead of driving your own car is a win for the environment.

#3 Sharing is caring

Do you live near a colleague? Perhaps you're heading to a dinner with a friend who lives down the road? Or maybe both your child and their friend next door are going to the same party? Reach out and set up a carpool – it's better for the environment and you get the added bonus of some friendly company. If you don't have anyone who lives near you or you're out and about, check out services like Uber and Lyft, or como.org.uk to discover carpool options.

#4 Choose public transport

Public transport is not always cheap, so check out any schemes that could make this option more affordable. Look for weekly, monthly or annual travelcards and see if there's an age-based discount card that you're eligible for. It's also worth getting in touch with your HR department to see if your company can help alleviate some of the financial burden, such as through a no-interest loan.

#5 Every little helps

If you can't ditch the car for your whole journey, then think about how you could drive part of the way. Maybe you can drive to the train station and then use public transport to complete your journey. You'll save on fuel too!

#6 While you're there...

One of the simplest ways of becoming an eco-friendly traveller every day is combining trips you might normally do separately. Pop to the shops on your way home, head to the gym *en route* to the supermarket.

#7 Savvy supermarkets

Do you get your groceries delivered? Great idea! The delivery vans act as buses for your food shopping, so it can be a much greener alternative if you're used to driving. Even better, look out for the 'eco' slots that many big supermarkets offer at peak times so the routes are efficient. Also, if available, opt out of plastic bags!

#8 Keep your car happy

If you have a car, look after it to ensure it is operating as efficiently as possible. Make sure you take it to be serviced regularly, that you use the right type of engine oil (you can check this in your handbook) and keep an eye on your tyre pressures.

#9 That's such a drag

Roof racks are really handy for when you're travelling but they're not necessary for driving to the nursery or gardening centre (probably). The racks ruin the streamlined design of your car and so contribute to inefficient fuel use. Bye bye, roof rack!

#10 What's in the trunk?

Similarly, if you have a car, make sure it's not overloaded. We're not talking people – it's good to carpool, after all – but do you really need twenty 2l bottles of water in your boot? What about those gym weights that never made it into the house…? The heavier your car, the more fuel it burns, so make sure you're only carrying what you need.

#11 Is it cold in here?

It's a summer's day. The sun is shining and the inside of your car feels like you've actually stepped onto the sun. As tempting as it might be to reach for that AC button, open your window instead. Of course, if you're blessed to live in a warm country, some days you might really need to use the AC, but by cutting down your use even a little bit, you're really helping out the planet.

#12 Unplug it

When you're travelling, it can be great to have electronic devices on hand – whether it's your satnav or your phone so you can get that roadtrip playlist going. But neither of these are really needed for your 30-minute commute. If you're not using them, unplug them and save the fuel (and the environment!).

#13 Stick to the speed limit

Of course we're not suggesting that you don't stick to the limit. But if you need any more incentive (other than it being a legal requirement) it's also much better for the environment. The US Department of Energy has claimed that aggressive driving (such as speeding or rapidly accelerating and braking) can lower your fuel mileage by up to 33 per cent![8] Sticking to the limit is safer, more fuel efficient and will save you money.

#14 Virtual meetings

We've come a long way from the days when you had to be physically in your office to do your work. Naturally, this isn't going to be possible for everyone, but if you have the option to work from home – do it! A study claims that if the UK doubled its number of people working from home by 2025, there would be over 370,000 fewer cars on the road, equivalent to around 420kg of CO2 emissions per person, per year.[9] Impressive.

#15 Pedal power

Alongside walking, cycling is the best way to travel since it emits no carbon emissions. If you live or work in a city, chances are you can rent a bike to get around, but do some research to see what bike-rental companies cater for your area. To get you started, Spinlister is a great platform where bike owners can advertise their bikes for renting. Grab your helmet and get going!

#16 Grab a ride

The modern (and safer) equivalent of hitchhiking, there are now many apps and platforms designed to make it easier to carpool with people you don't know. If this is something you're interested in, check out Blablacar, Liftshare and shareAcar.

#17 Walk-to-work week

Not only is this a great excuse to have a big stack of pancakes for breakfast, but walk-to-work week is a great way to start your day and even an opportunity to raise some money for charity (see the next tip). If your company doesn't already do one – take action! Get in touch with your manager and start the movement. For some support in doing this, check out walkit.com/walking-to-work

#18 Support fly-free charities

If you do organise a walk-to-work week or simply want to do a good deed, raise money for a charity focused on funding sustainable and carbon-efficient projects, such as the not-for-profit Cool Earth. They're committed to reducing carbon emissions – take a look at cooleffect.org.

#19 Responsible rubbish

We've all been there – you've left work but your stomach's already rumbling. It's a long journey home before dinner and you're getting hangrier by the second. You buy a snack (yum!) and now you're left with a can and a cardboard box. Instead of putting these in the bin on the train, take them home to recycle. Some train stations have recycling bins on the platforms, though, so keep an eye out for those too.

#20 Before you buy

When you're next buying a car, consider how to make the most eco-friendly choice. Opt for a car that's only as big as you need and keep in mind that four-wheel drive and automatic gearboxes use more fuel. Newer cars are also typically cleaner and more efficient. Check out online tools such as sust-it.net to check different models' fuel efficiency.

#21 Go car-free

But hang on a sec – do you even need a new car? A lot of us assume this will be cheaper than getting taxis or public transport, but if you travel infrequently, these might be more affordable (and cleaner) options.

#22 Be more informed

Lots of people are talking about sustainable travel nowadays and publishing brilliant and informative articles and books about it. Some great blogs to check out are: Charlie on Travel, Pebblemag and NOW.

#23 Get everyone involved

It's true that together we can achieve so much more than we could if we work alone, so get chatting to your friends and family. Talk about sustainable travel at dinner tonight or when you're having a tea break at work. The conversation starts here, with you.

PLANNING

#24 Location matters

One of the most powerful ways to travel (while also having a great time) is choosing locations to visit that are working to fight climate change and preserve their local ecosystems. Slovenia, Lake Tahoe, Ecuador and Portugal are just some of the places that are leading by example, but there are many more – check out the list at sustainabletop100.org for more inspiration.

#25 Social media

It's totally reasonable to want to travel somewhere because it's got beautiful views (hello, Grand Canyon) but don't choose your destination just because you've seen photos on social media. Consider the people you could meet, the places you could visit and the things you could do and eat. That way, you'll land on the destination that's perfect for the trip you want.

#26 Beware of over-tourism

Tourism can be integral to a country's economy. However, in some instances, too much tourism can be damaging to a country and its cultural sites. From overwhelming local people to ruining coastal environments or ancient ruins, there are a lot of places at risk of over-tourism. Madrid, New York, Machu Pichu and Bali are just a handful of destinations that have reported issues with over-tourism, so take a look at responsibletravel.com to find out more about other areas affected.

#27 Bring staycations back

We've become obsessed with leaving the country to have a great holiday, but there's so much to see on our own doorsteps. Are there any National Parks you can travel to, or historical cities you've always meant to visit? If you're based in the UK, there are numerous websites that will help you find beautiful walking routes that make brilliant days out – see walkit.com and Car Free Walks for some inspiration.

#28 Eco-friendly hotels

There are lots of fantastic hotels that are putting sustainability at the heart of their business, along with encouraging responsible tourism, good staff working conditions and community support. Check out their eco-credentials – in particular recycling and composting programmes, green cleaning products and renewable energy. For help with finding accommodation if you need a hand, check out: gstcouncil.org/for-travelers.

#29 Choose dorms

Not just for students, dorm rooms are a great way to meet people, save money and help save the planet. Just like on airplanes, more people in the same sized space means greater efficiency. Give it a go!

#30 Alternative accommodation

There are lots of options other than hotels which can be more eco-friendly. Choosing to stay in someone's spare room (through Airbnb or friends and family) is a fun option, or if you're feeling adventurous, you could also do a home exchange, couch surf or home stay. Check out greenvacatiohub.com for further ideas.

#31 Lights out!

Before you leave home (both when travelling and in your day-to-day routine), make sure to turn off all the lights. Even better, unplug all electronics. Appliances will continue to use electricity if plugged in and turned off – it's aptly called 'vampire' electricity – so save your money and the planet by unplugging everything before you head off.

#32 Turn down the thermostat

If you're not in the house, your heating does not need to be on full blast. Similarly, turn down your water heater if you have one.

#33 Pause the headlines

Make sure to pause any newspaper delivery subscriptions you are signed up to before you go on holiday. It'll save not only paper but the efforts of the person who delivers papers for your area.

#34 Don't chuck it – freeze it

It's a near-impossible task to eat everything from your fridge before you set off on holiday. But instead of throwing any leftovers away, see if you can freeze them, or if not, give them to your neighbours or colleagues. Except maybe that day-old tuna sandwich. That can go in the recycling…

#35 Embrace e-tickets

If offered to you, choose electronic tickets so you don't have to waste paper. Just remember to charge your phone before you leave the house!

#36 Responsible tours

When choosing a tour, it's best to do some thorough research. Check that the experience doesn't negatively impact local people or harm wildlife and be especially wary of animal-related tour experiences.

#37 Make a difference

If you're not fussed about having a holiday and more interested in travelling, see if there's a charity you could work with so that you can use your travelling to make a difference. A great example is WWOOF, when you can apply to work on a farm across the world. You could also volunteer to help with a charity abroad. Visit travel-peopleandplaces.co.uk for some helpful information on this.

#38 Research is cool

Before choosing your destination, make sure you know if it has any specific issues you should be aware of. For example, is the area prone to drought? If so, make sure to use water sparingly.

#39 Get to know the system

Avoid taking a taxi by looking up the public-transport system of the country you're visiting before you arrive. It's also worth checking out the most effective fare options, such as one-day passes or reloadable cards. They'll be much cheaper than getting taxis!

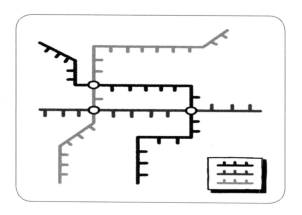

#40 Travel insurance

Insurance isn't the sexiest topic, but it is when you buy from companies such as Naturesave. They donate 10% of their income to environmental projects.

#41 Map it out

Plan your routes in advance to avoid getting lost. If you're going on a road trip, some satnavs offer an 'eco-friendly route', which calculates the most fuel-efficient journey you can take.

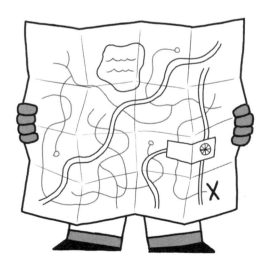

#42 Ask about your tours

If you're getting help with organising your holiday, make sure to ask your tour operator about environmentally friendly options. Never underestimate the power of the consumer!

#43 Travel out of season

This is a double win in our books. Not only can you avoid big crowds and long queues, but overcrowding has a negative impact on local habitats and wildlife (mainly through erosion and waste), so you'll be saving the environment too.

#44 Loyalty leverage

If you're a frequent traveller, your voice matters more to the big companies (both airlines and hotels). Research their company policies and be vocal about changes you want them to make and celebrate any moves in the right direction.

#45 Get inspired!

There are so many cool bloggers setting a great example for eco-friendly travel. If you're not sure where to begin, we'd recommend:

Every Steph
EcoTraveller
The Uprooted Rose
Small Footprints Big Adventures,
Ethical Traveller

#46 Take on the challenge

You're the competitive type, huh? Why not commit to a no-fly year and join in with the hashtag #nofly to find others doing their bit to save the world too.

PACKING

#47 Stay hydrated

Cut down on plastic by taking a reusable water bottle with you. A thermos and reusable straw are also handy for an eco-friendly traveller. If you're not able to drink the local water, invest in a water filter or water-purification tablets and use the RefillMyBottle app to find areas to top up during the day.

#48 Take a shopping bag

No intrepid explorer should be without a handy reusable shopping bag. Make sure to take yours with you. Who knows what exciting souvenirs or treats you'll want to buy?

#49 Second-hand suitcase

If you're in the market for a new suitcase, see if there are any preloved ones available nearby or online. You'll save money and help reduce waste. Top work!

#50 Multi-wear wardrobe

When choosing what clothes to take with you, go for items that don't need to be washed after just one wear and prioritise clothes that are quick dry, such as merino wool, bamboo and cotton.

#51 Borrow it

For some holidays and activities, you're going to need specific clothing and equipment (snorkelling gear and ski gloves, for example – although probably not at the same time). See if you can borrow any specialist clothes from friends and family first. It's much savvier than buying items you'll only use once.

#52 Refill, refill, refill

Instead of buying travel-sized products, invest in a reusable travel-sized container. This means you can refill it whenever you go on holiday and cut down on your plastic usage. Studies suggest that 15.5 million Brits buy travel-size bottles for their trips, leading to an estimated 980 tonnes of plastic being left at the end of holidays each year.[10] It's time to make a change.

#53 Protect the sea, too

Your skin needs protection from the sun, but avoid polluting the sea by choosing suntan lotions without oxybenzone and octinoxate in the ingredients – these are two chemicals that contribute to the bleaching of coral reefs.

#54 Take Tupperware

Avoid food waste by bringing your own Tupperware!
Take it to the next level by brining your own reusable
and/or recyclable cutlery and plates too.

#55 Remove packaging

Before dumping everything in your suitcase, get rid of any unnecessary packaging. It's easier to recycle waste materials at home and you'll be travelling lighter – double eco-points!

#56 Pack with purpose

If you are taking a big bag, include some items that will make a difference to the communities you're visiting. Pack for a Purpose is a brilliant organisation that let's you know what items are needed and where you can donate them. Check out their website before your next trip.

#57 Double up

Be an especially savvy packer by choosing pieces that have multiple uses. For example, a sarong can also be used as a scarf, towel and blanket.

#58 Get 'appy

There are loads of really helpful apps to make sustainable travel simpler – Green Globe is useful for finding eco-friendly accommodation and attractions, while HopStop provides invaluable information about getting around cities.

#59 Leave your books on the shelf

Now, we're not suggesting you ditch books completely (obviously), but when you're travelling it's a great idea to take an e-reader instead. They weigh less and are generally more convenient when you're out and about.

#60 Rent on location

Taking specialist equipment with you involves more fuel, whatever your mode of transport (unless you plan on walking to your destination), so rent when you get there. This goes for skis, surfing board, ice skates, camping equipment and more.

TO FLY

OR NOT

TO FLY?

#61 Follow the 3-hour rule

If it would take you less than 3 hours to fly to your destination, look at alternative options (train or boat, for example). Following this rule is a simple way to make sure you're not flying unnecessarily.

#62 Full steam ahead!

Well, not steam any more – that's not very environmentally friendly either. But trains are having a comeback. Studies have shown that taking the train to Paris instead of the plane can cut your CO_2 emissions by up to ninety per cent.[11] Not only this, but the experience is often less stressful (fewer queues), you get more leg room, you can walk around during the journey and you can really connect to the surroundings you're travelling through. Choo choo!

#63 All about the train

There are so many countries that are perfectly suited to travelling through by train. Make your train journey the focus of your travelling and choose some of the world's most magnificent routes for your holiday. Get online to find more about interrailing and other train routes.

#64 Fuss-free travelling

Travelling by train doesn't need to be complicated. Mark Smith has done all the hard work and his blog seat61.com has everything you need for planning a train-based holiday. You'll find tips and tricks for taking trains across the world, so no more excuses!

#65 Be adventurous

There are so many exciting ways to get around cities and many of them will be far more memorable than hopping in a taxi or renting a car. Look for electric-assisted bikes, tuk tuks, electric scooters and Segways for fun ways to get around without walking for hours.

#66 Rent it right

If you need to rent a car to get where you need to go, choose an agency that offers an electric or hybrid option. Also look for other details, such as its fuel efficiency and whether the car has rooftop solar panels.

#67 Rocking road trips

Lots of car-rental agencies need their cars moved from one of their locations to another, so will offer you significantly cheaper options for one-way journeys. This is better for the environment too, since you'll be moving a car that would have ended up being driven there anyway. Win win!

#68 A to B(us)

Not just for the commute, travelling longer distances by bus and coach can be a more eco-friendly way to travel. You don't need to check in as early as flights, tickets are cheaper and if you're not the plan-three-months-in-advance type, you often don't need a booking. From regional to international, there are lots of options.

#69 Cargo go go!

This might seem very 'out there', but travelling by cargo ship is becoming more and more popular. Specific travel agents (visit langsamreisen.de) are now offering the spare cabin space on ships (including sailing boats, freighter and mail ships) to members of the public. Granted, it will take you longer than flying, there's less choice and journeys are currently considerably more expensive. However if you're looking for something different – this definitely is it.

#70 Cross-country cycling

It's time to get your heart pumping. Truly experience a landscape by getting on your bike and cycling to your destination. You'll likely find some hidden gems, all the while avoiding all the other tourists. Dreamy.

#71 Let's go cruising

The cruise industry is growing at a remarkable rate. It's the fastest-growing sector for the past twenty years with over 28 million passengers choosing this mode of transport in 2018.[12] However, it's estimated that the average cruise-ship passenger emits the equivalent carbon emissions of a return economy flight from London to Tokyo.[13] So, if possible, choose to travel by regular ferries instead of cruise liners.

#72 Go direct!

But sometimes, you just have to fly. If this is the case, when possible, always opt for direct flights (or at least the fewest number of stops). Planes use a huge amount of fuel for take-off and landing, so by choosing a route that avoids stopovers, you'll be making an eco-friendlier choice.

#73 Eco Economy

While we typically aspire towards flying business or first class, it turns out that flying economy is much better for the environment. Seats in the higher classes use up far more space than in economy and research by the World Bank in 2013 estimates that on average the carbon-emissions footprint per passenger in business is three times that of an economy passenger and first class is *nine* times bigger.[14] It's time to embrace economy!

#74 Pack light

Do you really need that big ol' suitcase for a long weekend away? Grab a rucksack and with some savvy packing (check out Youtube for some whizzy space-saving ways to fold your clothes) you'll be able to fit in much more than you realise. If you're travelling with others, see if you can share a luggage bag too. You'll save money and the limited space will ensure you're only taking what you need.

#75 Split it up

If you're planning on moving around during your holiday, look at how you can divide your journey so you can take more environmentally friendly forms of transport. If you need to fly initially, use the 30-minute rule (see page 8) to then figure out if you could travel by train, coach or bus to your next destination. If you're a sporty type, perhaps you could even cycle?

#76 Co-ordinate your flights

If you're travelling with others, try to pick the same flights. This way, you can share your transfer to your accommodation, or even share a rental car.

#77 Turn down the taxi

Don't automatically head for the taxi queue as soon as you land – instead, think ahead and plan an eco-friendly route from the airport. Many airports run a shuttle service into the city centre (use shuttlefinder. com to help you with this) and local bus and train options are not only greener but often much cheaper.

#78 Know your airlines

When picking your flight, try to go with the most environmentally friendly airline you can. Atomsfair has pulled together their 'Airline Index' that lists all the major airlines and puts them in order of carbon emissions produced – check it out at atmosfair.de

#79 Carbon offset it

The conversation around carbon offsetting is complex (see page 3), but to help you figure out the best carbon-offsetting programme for you, here are some questions to ask:

Where is my money going?
How much of my money goes to the project?
What will it be used for?
How much of the project is funded by carbon offsetting?

#80 Offsetting tools

There are loads of online tools that will help you offset your carbon emissions. It's best to do some research to find the one that best suits your aims, but here are three to get your started:

1. **The World Land Trust** – funds conservation projects that help protect and restore tropical habitats.
2. **Atmosfair** – offers carbon-efficient projects you can donate to.
3. **Cool Effect** – helps you offset not just your carbon-dioxide emissions but also your methane and nitrous-oxide footprints.

WHEN YOU

GET THERE

#81 Take the oath!

In 2017 Palau made history by being the first country to require visitors to sign a pledge when they got to Customs, promising to protect Palau's land.[15] It inspired both Iceland and New Zealand to follow suit, and while many countries still don't have this formal commitment, it's worth making one yourself whenever you visit somewhere new, as a reminder to be respectful not just of the people but also the place you are visiting.

#82 Always stick to the path

There's so much to see when you're out and about, but when you're hiking, make sure you always stick to the path. Wandering off the beaten track might seem adventurous, but you risk hurting local wildlife and ecosystems, so it's a big no.

#83 Switch it off

As you would at home, turn off lights, heating and air conditioning when you don't need them.

#84 Do Not Disturb!

Hotels often clean your room far more often than you need. Put your 'Do Not Disturb' sign to good use to limit the number of times your bed sheets are changed and your room is tidied.

#85 Limit your towels

If you think your laundry pile at home is big, take a moment to consider how big a hotel's laundry pile must be. Washing all the bed linen and towels takes a lot of energy, so use your towels mindfully and reuse them like you would at home.

#86 Eat local...

One of the most powerful and simplest things you can do on holiday is practise lower carbon impact eating. In essence, this means choosing local and organic food as much as possible. It means the produce has travelled fewer miles and is likely to be less processed. (It'll probably taste better too!)

#87 ...and drink local

Of course, no holiday is complete without a cheeky drink. Similarly, choose local craft brews, wines and spirits.

#88 Don't get hangry

We can start off the holiday with good intentions, but let's face it, if you get hangry (aka hungry and angry) you'll end up going to the first familiar chain restaurant you see. At the beginning of your holiday, ask your host for some local recommendations, so you have options at the ready after a long day.

#89 Veggie goodness

We're becoming more aware of the health benefits of plant-based diets, but eating your veg is generally better for the planet too. Why not have a go at being vegetarian for your holiday? You'll be surprised how many tasty dishes there are on the menu that you wouldn't have considered before…

#90 Ready to cook?

You might not be the handiest in the kitchen, but choosing to self-cater while you're on holiday is a move in the sustainable direction. It gives you more control over the produce you eat (check out pages 103-6) and you'll save money too. Challenge yourself to eat out only once a day.

#91 Choosing activities

Go for net positive impact activities when you're on holiday. This includes choosing walking or cycling tours instead of bus ones, shopping at independent rather than chain retailers, and shopping and cooking like a local instead of heading to your favourite restaurant brand that you can get at home.

#92 Avoid mass-produced souvenirs

Often souvenirs that are produced on a large scale have been transported from another country. Instead, look out for gems created by local artisans – they'll be much more evocative of the place you've visited and you'll be helping the local economy.

#93 Don't litter

You wouldn't want someone throwing rubbish in your garden, so don't do it when you're on holiday. Enough said.

#94 Pick it up

It's very easy to just walk past litter on the floor, but next time you see some, do your good deed of the day and pick it up and throw it away. If you have children with you, make it into a game – whoever can throw away the most rubbish by the end of the holiday wins a prize.

#95 Return maps

If they're in good condition still by the end of your holiday, return your maps and leaflets to the front desk.

#96 Take your toiletries

Make sure to take any of the complementary toiletries that you've opened but not finished using, home with you. Otherwise they'll just be thrown away and wasted.

#97 Check recycling options

Lots of countries have recycling systems nowadays, so ask your accommodation provider what the rules are. This is especially useful if you're self-catering, where you'll end up with food and packaging waste.

#98 Label your leftovers

It's impossible to use up all your leftovers at the end of the holiday. For anything that won't make a good snack for the trip, label it with the date you opened the product and leave it in the fridge. This means that the owner or cleaner is informed once you've left and might be able to use it instead.

#99 Speedy showers

If you haven't already, it's time to master the power shower. Shorter washes mean less water and so are better for the environment. Simple.

#100 Give feedback

After your holiday, make sure to leave feedback for your providers. This can be compliments or constructive criticism – both are helpful for celebrating or encouraging eco-friendly change.

#101 Spread the word!

Now that you know everything about being a sustainable traveller, go tell people! People are much more likely to make a change if they get a personal recommendation, so choose your favourite few tips and share the wisdom. If you're on Twitter, let us know by using the hashtag #FkFlying.

REFERENCES

1   https://www.statista.com/statistics/200002/international-car-sales-since-1990/ (accessed 02/03).
2   https://www.statista.com/statistics/564769/airline-industry-number-of-flights/ (accessed 02/03).
3   https://www.earth-changers.com/blog/2018/5/15/10-tips-on-how-to-reduce-your-carbon-footprint-in-travel-and-should-you-carbon-offset (Accessed 09/02).
4   https://www.iata.org/en/pressroom/pr/2018-10-24-02 (access 02/03).
5   https://www.theguardian.com/environment/ng-interactive/2019/jul/19/carbon-calculator-how-taking-one-flight-emits-as-much-as-many-people-do-in-a-year (accessed 02/03).
6   https://www.theforgottensolution.org/ (Accessed 09/02).
7   https://www.greenchoices.org/green-living/transport/introduction (accessed 09/02).
8   https://www.prevention.com/health/g20492347/70-easy-ways-to-green-up-your-life/ (accessed 09/02).
9   https://airqualitynews.com/2019/04/24/working-from-home-could-significantly-reduce-uks-co2-emissions/ (accessed 29/02).
10 https://www.directlinegroup.co.uk/en/news/brand-news/2018/plastic-waste--980-tonnes-of-travel-sized-products-are-dumped-ev.html (accessed 29/02).
11 https://www.seat61.com/CO2flights.htm (accessed 09/02).
12 https://www.greenchoices.org/eco-holidays/eco-holiday-choices/environmental-impact-of-holidays (accessed 09/02).
13 https://www.tourismdashboard.org/explore-the-data/cruise-ship/ (accessed 02/03).
14 https://www.earth-changers.com/blog/2018/5/15/10-tips-on-how-to-reduce-your-carbon-footprint-in-travel-and-should-you-carbon-offset (accessed 09/02).
15 Read more about Palau's Pledge at palaupledge.com